HAL•LEONARD

JAZZ PLAY-ALONG®

Book and CD for B♭, E♭, C and Bass Clef Instruments

volume 114

MODERN JAZZ QUARTET
FAVORITES
10 CLASSIC TUNES

Arranged and Produced by
Mark Taylor and Jim Roberts

BOOK

CD

Cover photo © Enid Farber / Retna Ltd.

ISBN 978-1-4234-8356-4

HAL•LEONARD®
CORPORATION
7777 W. BLUEMOUND RD. P.O.Box 13819 MILWAUKEE, WI 53213

Visit Hal Leonard Online at
www.halleonard.com

MODERN JAZZ QUARTET FAVORITES

HAL•LEONARD
JAZZ PLAY-ALONG

Volume 114

Arranged and Produced by
Mark Taylor and Jim Roberts

Featured Players:

Graham Breedlove–Trumpet
John Desalme–Tenor Sax
Tony Nalker–Piano
Jim Roberts–Guitar and Bass
Todd Harrison–Drums

**Recorded at Bias Studios, Springfield, Virginia
Bob Dawson, Engineer**

HOW TO USE THE CD:

Each song has <u>two</u> tracks:

1) Split Track/Melody

Woodwind, Brass, Keyboard, and **Mallet Players** can use this track as a learning tool for melody style and inflection.

Bass Players can learn and perform with this track – remove the recorded bass track by turning down the volume on the LEFT channel.

Keyboard and **Guitar Players** can learn and perform with this track – remove the recorded piano part by turning down the volume on the RIGHT channel.

2) Full Stereo Track

Soloists or **Groups** can learn and perform with this accompaniment track with the RHYTHM SECTION only.

AFTERNOON IN PARIS

BY JOHN LEWIS

C VERSION

MEDIUM SWING

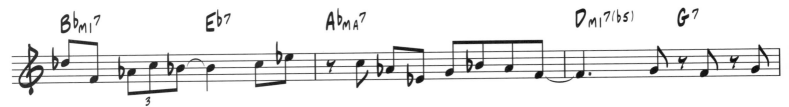

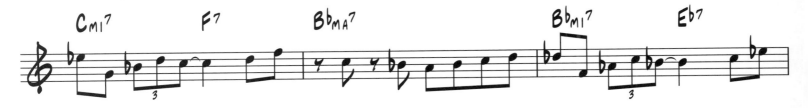

TO CODA

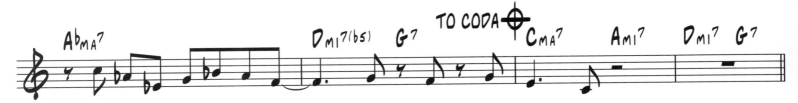

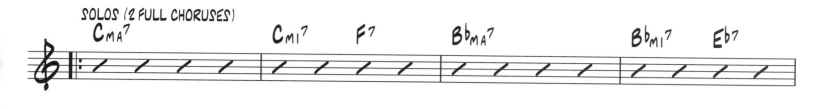

SOLOS (2 FULL CHORUSES)

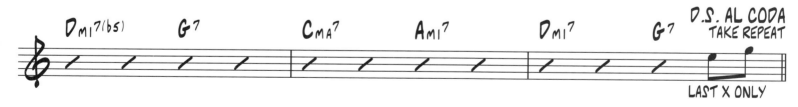

BAGS' GROOVE

C VERSION

BY MILT JACKSON

CD
◆5 : SPLIT TRACK/MELODY
◆6 : FULL STEREO TRACK

CONNIE'S BLUES

BY MILT JACKSON

C VERSION

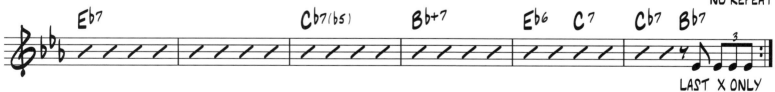

THE JASMINE TREE

BY JOHN LEWIS

C VERSION

MILANO

BY JOHN LEWIS

C VERSION

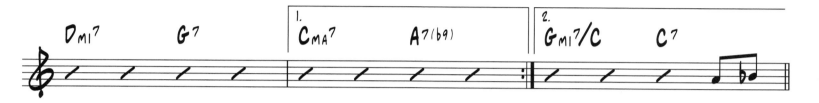

THE QUEEN'S FANCY

BY JOHN LEWIS

Reunion Blues

BY MILT JACKSON

C VERSION

CD
19: SPLIT TRACK/MELODY
20: FULL STEREO TRACK

TWO DEGREES EAST, THREE DEGREES WEST

BY JOHN LEWIS

C VERSION

CD
15 : SPLIT TRACK/MELODY
16 : FULL STEREO TRACK

SKATING IN CENTRAL PARK

BY JOHN LEWIS

C VERSION

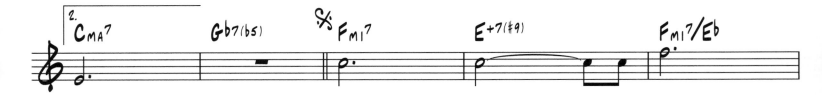

CD

A SOCIAL CALL

BY JOHN LEWIS

C VERSION

MEDIUM SWING

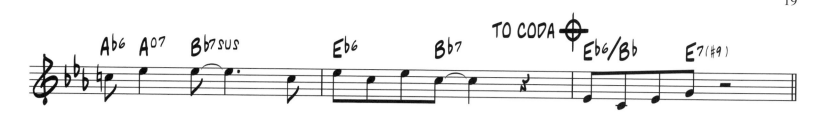

AFTERNOON IN PARIS

BY JOHN LEWIS

Bb VERSION

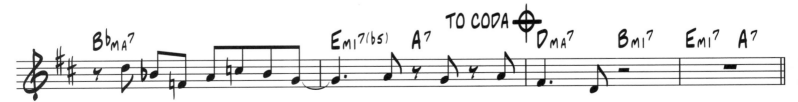

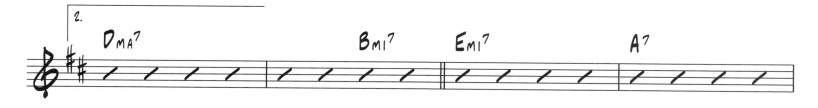

BAGS' GROOVE

By Milt Jackson

Bb VERSION

CD
- **5**: SPLIT TRACK/MELODY
- **6**: FULL STEREO TRACK

CONNIE'S BLUES

BY MILT JACKSON

Bb VERSION

SLOW SWING

THE JASMINE TREE

BY JOHN LEWIS

Bb VERSION

Milano

BY JOHN LEWIS

CD
- **9** : SPLIT TRACK/MELODY
- **10** : FULL STEREO TRACK

Bb VERSION

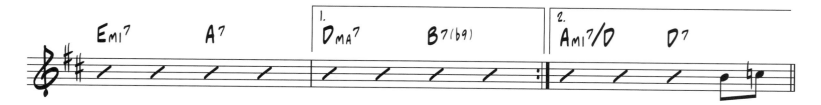

THE QUEEN'S FANCY

BY JOHN LEWIS

Reunion Blues

BY MILT JACKSON

CD
19 : SPLIT TRACK/MELODY
20 : FULL STEREO TRACK

TWO DEGREES EAST, THREE DEGREES WEST

BY JOHN LEWIS

Bb VERSION

MEDIUM SWING

SOLOS (7 CHORUSES)

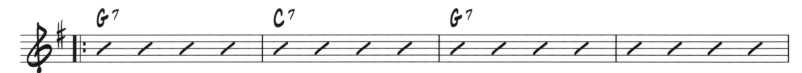

CD

15: SPLIT TRACK/MELODY
16: FULL STEREO TRACK

SKATING IN CENTRAL PARK

BY JOHN LEWIS

Bb Version

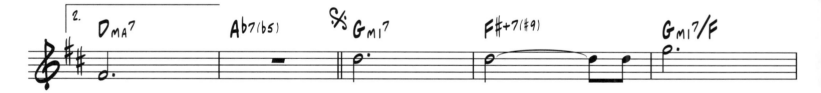

CD

A SOCIAL CALL

BY JOHN LEWIS

Bb VERSION

CD

AFTERNOON IN PARIS

BY JOHN LEWIS

Eb VERSION

MEDIUM SWING

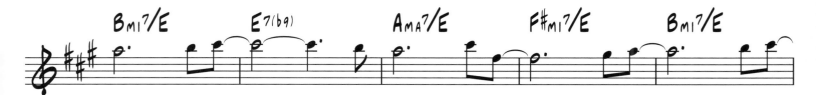

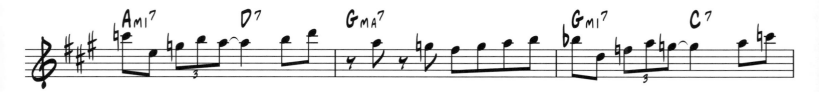

TO CODA ⊕

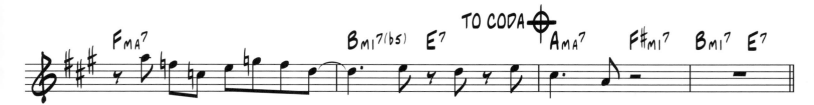

SOLOS (2 FULL CHORUSES)

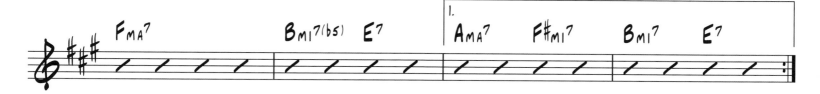

D.S. AL CODA
TAKE REPEAT

LAST X ONLY

CD

③ : SPLIT TRACK/MELODY
④ : FULL STEREO TRACK

BAGS' GROOVE

Eb VERSION

BY MILT JACKSON

CONNIE'S BLUES

BY MILT JACKSON

CD
◆ : SPLIT TRACK/MELODY
◆ : FULL STEREO TRACK

Eb VERSION

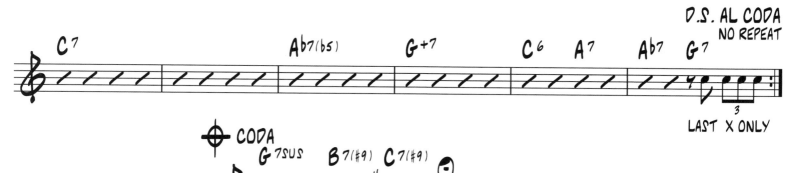

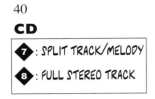

THE JASMINE TREE

BY JOHN LEWIS

Eb VERSION

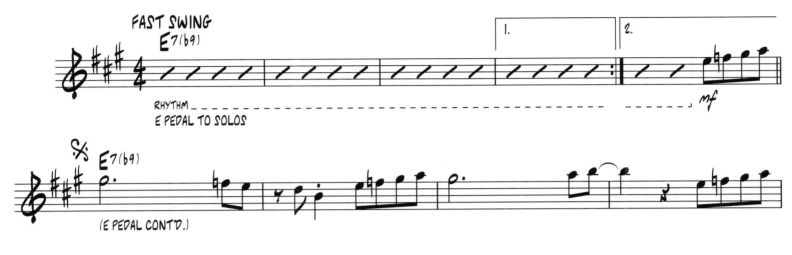

41

Milano

BY JOHN LEWIS

THE QUEEN'S FANCY

BY JOHN LEWIS

Eb VERSION

45

Reunion Blues

BY MILT JACKSON

Eb VERSION

TWO DEGREES EAST, THREE DEGREES WEST

CD
19: SPLIT TRACK/MELODY
20: FULL STEREO TRACK

BY JOHN LEWIS

Eb VERSION

MEDIUM SWING

SKATING IN CENTRAL PARK

BY JOHN LEWIS

Eb VERSION

MEDIUM WALTZ

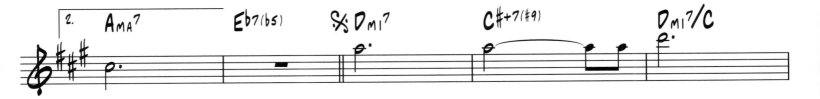

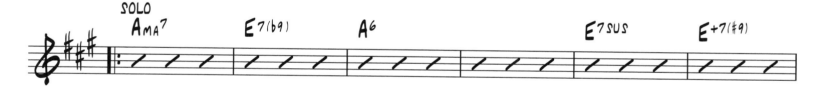

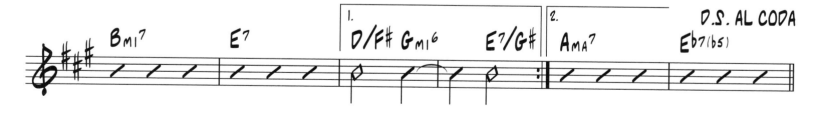

A SOCIAL CALL

BY JOHN LEWIS

CD
17: SPLIT TRACK/MELODY
18: FULL STEREO TRACK

Eb VERSION

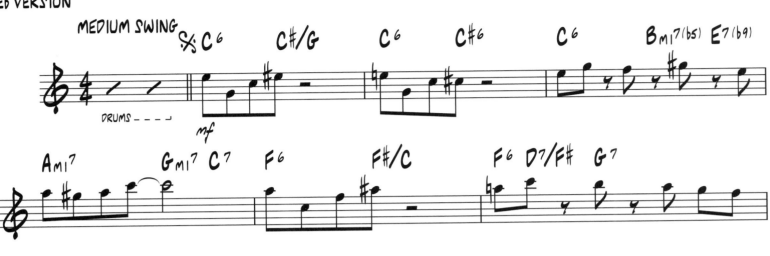

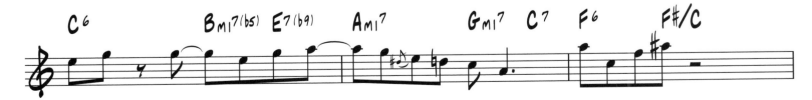

CD

1 : SPLIT TRACK/MELODY
2 : FULL STEREO TRACK

AFTERNOON IN PARIS

BY JOHN LEWIS

𝄢 : C VERSION

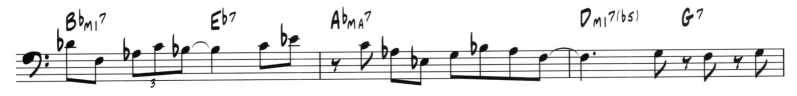

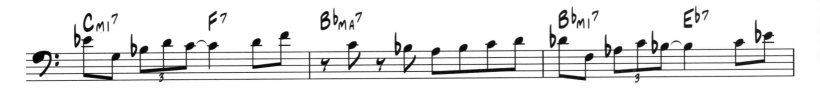

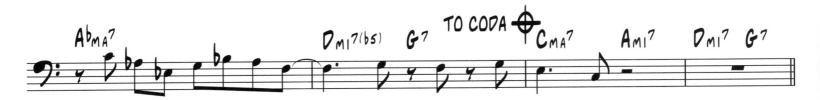

SOLOS (2 FULL CHORUSES)

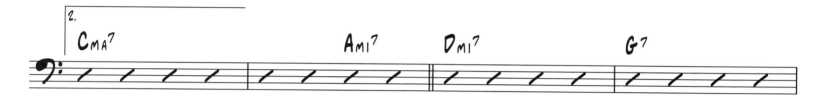

D.S. AL CODA
TAKE REPEAT

LAST X ONLY

CODA

BAGS' GROOVE

BY MILT JACKSON

𝄢: C VERSION

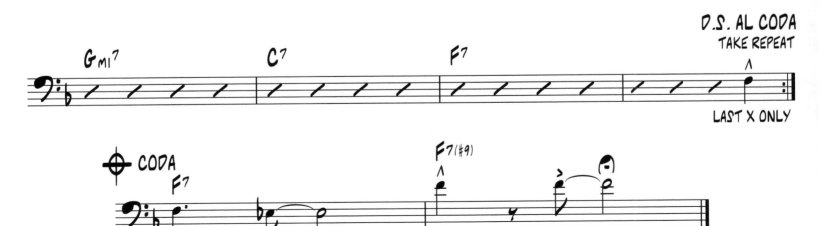

CONNIE'S BLUES

BY MILT JACKSON

𝄢: C VERSION

THE JASMINE TREE

BY JOHN LEWIS

CD
7 : SPLIT TRACK/MELODY
8 : FULL STEREO TRACK

𝄢: C VERSION

Milano

BY JOHN LEWIS

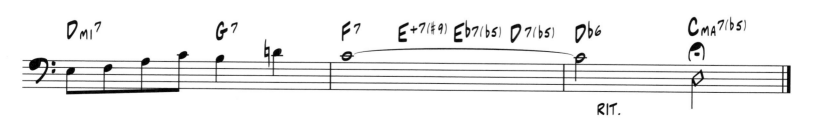

THE QUEEN'S FANCY

By John Lewis

REUNION BLUES

BY MILT JACKSON

𝄢: C VERSION

TWO DEGREES EAST, THREE DEGREES WEST

BY JOHN LEWIS

CD
- **19** : SPLIT TRACK/MELODY
- **20** : FULL STEREO TRACK

𝄢: C VERSION

MEDIUM SWING

FINE

SOLOS (7 CHORUSES)

D.C. AL FINE

CD
- **15** : SPLIT TRACK/MELODY
- **16** : FULL STEREO TRACK

SKATING IN CENTRAL PARK

BY JOHN LEWIS

𝄢: C VERSION

MEDIUM WALTZ

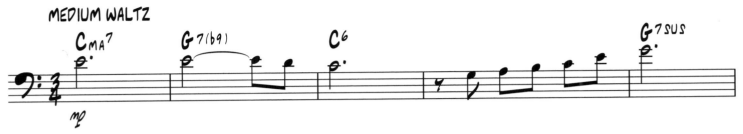

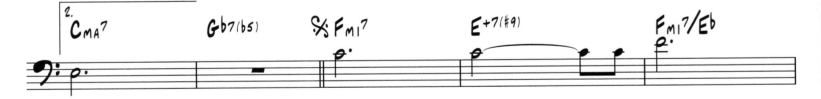

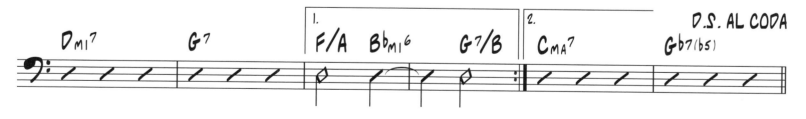

CD

A SOCIAL CALL

BY JOHN LEWIS

𝄢: C VERSION

Presenting the Hal Leonard JAZZ PLAY-ALONG SERIES

For use with all B-flat, E-flat, Bass Clef and C instruments, the Jazz Play-Along® Series is the ultimate learning tool for all jazz musicians. With musician-friendly lead sheets, melody cues, and other split-track choices on the included CD, these first-of-a-kind packages help you master improvisation while playing some of the greatest tunes of all time. FOR STUDY, each tune includes a split track with: melody cue with proper style and inflection • professional rhythm tracks • choruses for soloing • removable bass part • removable piano part. FOR PERFORMANCE, each tune also has: an additional full stereo accompaniment track (no melody) • additional choruses for soloing.

1. DUKE ELLINGTON
00841644 .... $16.95

2. MILES DAVIS
00841645 .... $16.95

3. THE BLUES
00841646 .... $16.99

4. JAZZ BALLADS
00841691 .... $16.99

5. BEST OF BEBOP
00841689 .... $16.99

6. JAZZ CLASSICS WITH EASY CHANGES
00841690 .... $16.99

7. ESSENTIAL JAZZ STANDARDS
00843000 .... $16.99

8. ANTONIO CARLOS JOBIM AND THE ART OF THE BOSSA NOVA
00843001 .... $16.95

9. DIZZY GILLESPIE
00843002 .... $16.99

10. DISNEY CLASSICS
00843003 .... $16.99

11. RODGERS AND HART FAVORITES
00843004 .... $16.99

12. ESSENTIAL JAZZ CLASSICS
00843005 .... $16.99

13. JOHN COLTRANE
00843006 .... $16.95

14. IRVING BERLIN
00843007 .... $15.99

15. RODGERS & HAMMERSTEIN
00843008 .... $15.99

16. COLE PORTER
00843009 .... $15.95

17. COUNT BASIE
00843010 .... $16.95

18. HAROLD ARLEN
00843011 .... $15.95

19. COOL JAZZ
00843012 .... $15.95

20. CHRISTMAS CAROLS
00843080 .... $14.95

21. RODGERS AND HART CLASSICS
00843014 .... $14.95

22. WAYNE SHORTER
00843015 .... $16.95

23. LATIN JAZZ
00843016 .... $16.95

24. EARLY JAZZ STANDARDS
00843017 .... $14.95

25. CHRISTMAS JAZZ
00843018 .... $16.95

26. CHARLIE PARKER
00843019 .... $16.95

27. GREAT JAZZ STANDARDS
00843020 .... $15.99

28. BIG BAND ERA
00843021 .... $15.99

29. LENNON AND MCCARTNEY
00843022 .... $16.95

30. BLUES' BEST
00843023 .... $15.99

31. JAZZ IN THREE
00843024 .... $15.99

32. BEST OF SWING
00843025 .... $15.99

33. SONNY ROLLINS
00843029 .... $15.95

34. ALL TIME STANDARDS
00843030 .... $15.99

35. BLUESY JAZZ
00843031 .... $15.99

36. HORACE SILVER
00843032 .... $16.95

37. BILL EVANS
00843033 .... $16.95

38. YULETIDE JAZZ
00843034 .... $16.95

39. "ALL THE THINGS YOU ARE" & MORE JEROME KERN SONGS
00843035 .... $15.99

40. BOSSA NOVA
00843036 .... $15.99

41. CLASSIC DUKE ELLINGTON
00843037 .... $16.99

42. GERRY MULLIGAN FAVORITES
00843038 .... $16.99

43. GERRY MULLIGAN CLASSICS
00843039 .... $16.95

44. OLIVER NELSON
00843040 .... $16.95

45. JAZZ AT THE MOVIES
00843041 .... $15.99

46. BROADWAY JAZZ STANDARDS
00843042 .... $15.99

47. CLASSIC JAZZ BALLADS
00843043 .... $15.99

48. BEBOP CLASSICS
00843044 .... $16.99

49. MILES DAVIS STANDARDS
00843045 .... $16.95

50. GREAT JAZZ CLASSICS
00843046 .... $15.99

51. UP-TEMPO JAZZ
00843047 .... $15.99

52. STEVIE WONDER
00843048 .... $15.95

53. RHYTHM CHANGES
00843049 .... $15.99

Prices, contents, and availability subject to change without notice.

FOR MORE INFORMATION, SEE YOUR LOCAL MUSIC DEALER, OR WRITE TO:

HAL•LEONARD® CORPORATION
7777 W. BLUEMOUND RD. P.O. BOX 13819
MILWAUKEE, WISCONSIN 53213

For complete songlists and more, visit Hal Leonard online at
www.halleonard.com

0809

Jazz Instruction & Improvisation

Books for All Instruments from Hal Leonard

AN APPROACH TO JAZZ IMPROVISATION
by Dave Pozzi
Musicians Institute Press
Explore the styles of Charlie Parker, Sonny Rollins, Bud Powell and others with this comprehensive guide to jazz improvisation. Covers: scale choices • chord analysis • phrasing • melodies • harmonic progressions • more.
00695135 Book/CD Pack $17.95

BUILDING A JAZZ VOCABULARY
By Mike Steinel
A valuable resource for learning the basics of jazz from Mike Steinel of the University of North Texas. It covers: the basics of jazz • how to build effective solos • a comprehensive practice routine • and a jazz vocabulary of the masters.
00849911 ....$19.95

THE CYCLE OF FIFTHS
by Emile and Laura De Cosmo
This essential instruction book provides more than 450 exercises, including hundreds of melodic and rhythmic ideas. The book is designed to help improvisors master the cycle of fifths, one of the primary progressions in music. Guaranteed to refine technique, enhance improvisational fluency, and improve sight-reading!
00311114 ....$16.99

THE DIATONIC CYCLE
by Emile and Laura De Cosmo
Renowned jazz educators Emile and Laura De Cosmo provide more than 300 exercises to help improvisors tackle one of music's most common progressions: the diatonic cycle. This book is guaranteed to refine technique, enhance improvisational fluency, and improve sight-reading!
00311115 ....$16.95

EAR TRAINING
by Keith Wyatt,
Carl Schroeder and Joe Elliott
Musicians Institute Press
Covers: basic pitch matching • singing major and minor scales • identifying intervals • transcribing melodies and rhythm • identifying chords and progressions • seventh chords and the blues • modal interchange, chromaticism, modulation • and more.
00695198 Book/2-CD Pack.....................$24.95

EXERCISES AND ETUDES FOR THE JAZZ INSTRUMENTALIST
by J.J. Johnson
Designed as study material and playable by any instrument, these pieces run the gamut of the jazz experience, featuring common and uncommon time signatures and keys, and styles from ballads to funk. They are progressively graded so that both beginners and professionals will be challenged by the demands of this wonderful music.
00842018 Bass Clef Edition....................$16.95
00842042 Treble Clef Edition.................$16.95

JAZZOLOGY
THE ENCYCLOPEDIA OF JAZZ THEORY FOR ALL MUSICIANS
by Robert Rawlins and
Nor Eddine Bahha
This comprehensive resource covers a variety of jazz topics, for beginners and pros of any instrument. The book serves as an encyclopedia for reference, a thorough methodology for the student, and a workbook for the classroom.
00311167 ....$18.95

JAZZ THEORY RESOURCES
by Bert Ligon
Houston Publishing, Inc.
This is a jazz theory text in two volumes. **Volume 1 includes:** review of basic theory • rhythm in jazz performance • triadic generalization • diatonic harmonic progressions and analysis • substitutions and turnarounds • and more. **Volume 2 includes:** modes and modal frameworks • quartal harmony • extended tertian structures and triadic superimposition • pentatonic applications • coloring "outside" the lines and beyond • and more.
00030458 Volume 1...............................$39.95
00030459 Volume 2..............................$29.95

JOY OF IMPROV
by Dave Frank and John Amaral
This book/CD course on improvisation for all instruments and all styles will help players develop monster musical skills! **Book One** imparts a solid basis in technique, rhythm, chord theory, ear training and improv concepts. **Book Two** explores more advanced chord voicings, chord arranging techniques and more challenging blues and melodic lines. The CD can be used as a listening and play-along tool.
00220005 Book 1 – Book/CD Pack $24.95
00220006 Book 2 – Book/CD Pack $24.95

THE PATH TO JAZZ IMPROVISATION
by Emile and Laura De Cosmo
This fascinating jazz instruction book offers an innovative, scholarly approach to the art of improvisation. It includes in-depth analysis and lessons about: cycle of fifths • diatonic cycle • overtone series • pentatonic scale • harmonic and melodic minor scale • polytonal order of keys • blues and bebop scales • modes • and more.
00310904 ....$14.95

THE SOURCE
THE DICTIONARY OF CONTEMPORARY AND TRADITIONAL SCALES
by Steve Barta
This book serves as an informative guide for people who are looking for good, solid information regarding scales, chords, and how they work together. It provides right and left hand fingerings for scales, chords, and complete inversions. Includes over 20 different scales, each written in all 12 keys.
00240885 ....$15.95

21 BEBOP EXERCISES
by Steve Rawlins
This book/CD pack is both a warm-up collection and a manual for bebop phrasing. Its tasty and sophisticated exercises will help you develop your proficiency with jazz interpretation. It concentrates on practice in all twelve keys — moving higher by half-step — to help develop dexterity and range. The companion CD includes all of the exercises in 12 keys.
00315341 Book/CD Pack $17.95

THE WOODSHEDDING SOURCE BOOK
by Emile De Cosmo
Rehearsing with this method daily will improve technique, reading ability, rhythmic and harmonic vocabulary, eye/finger coordination, endurance, range, theoretical knowledge, and listening skills – all of which lead to superior improvisational skills.
00842000 C Instruments $19.95

FOR MORE INFORMATION, SEE YOUR LOCAL MUSIC DEALER, OR WRITE TO:

7777 W. BLUEMOUND RD. P.O. BOX 13819 MILWAUKEE, WI 53213

Prices, contents & availability subject to change without notice.

Visit Hal Leonard online at
www.halleonard.com

0409